Maintaining
Balance in a
Stress-filled World

MIDGE DeSART

Regular Baptist Press
1300 North Meacham Road
Schaumburg, Illinois 60173-4806

MAINTAINING BALANCE IN A STRESS-FILLED WORLD
© 2003
Regular Baptist Press • Schaumburg, Illinois
1-800-727-4440
www.regularbaptistpress.org

RBP5291 • ISBN: 0-87227-984-7

Contents

Preface 7

Lesson 1   Stressed? Who's Stressed? 9

Lesson 2   In His Care 19

Lesson 3   Who Am I, Really? 29

Lesson 4   I Don't Want to Be Like That 35

Lesson 5   The Gift of Pain 41

Lesson 6   Is He Listening? 49

Lesson 7   Kept in the Palm of His Hand 57

Lesson 8   Bad News, Good News 65

Lesson 9   Serendipity 71

Lesson 10 God Is Big Enough 77

Conclusion 83

Leader's Guide 85

Dedication

To my husband, Keith, who has shown me what
unconditional love is.

Preface

THE COLORS AREN'T quite right. What's the problem? Move the green square to the other side. That's it! A small change made the difference. Now the pattern is just right. It's all a matter of balance.

Have you ever had too much of a good thing? A little cake is wonderful. It leaves you wanting more. So you decide to take the corner piece—the one with all the frosting. Yum! Mouthful by mouthful you devour the frosting until you find yourself scraping the frosting away from the cake in disgust. You can't eat another bite of frosting. You've had way too much of a good thing.

Balance.

Picture yourself placing one foot carefully in front of the other on a balance beam. If you shift your weight ever so slightly, you could fall off. It's all a matter of balance.

How can we maintain *balance* in a stress-filled world?

Me? Stressed? Of course not. I'm a Christian, and Peter told us Christians to cast "all your care upon him; for he careth for you" (1 Peter 5:7). We can be stressed to the blowing point and not realize that we have a problem.

How can we identify stress? It's an important question. Then, after we have identified stress, what can we do about it? Sometimes there seems to be no way out of a bad situation. But Scripture has a lot to say about coping with stress.

The lessons in this book deal with high-stress areas of life: the birth of a child, losing a job, the death of a loved one—each one is a life-changing event.

The Christian woman has a lifeline to the Creator of life. James 4:8 states, "Draw nigh to God, and he will draw nigh to you." Hebrews 4:16 encourages us to "come boldly unto the throne of grace, that we may obtain mercy, and find grace to help in time of need."

God has provided in His Word the answers to life's struggles. Let's take a look.

Stressed? Who's Stressed?

I T'S 10:00 A.M. The five-year-old is in school until 11:00. The one-year-old is taking a nap, and the three-year-old is screaming at the top of her lungs because she just spilled her milk. Elaine is on her hands and knees, wiping up the milk when the phone rings. She answers, trying to sound cheerful above the wailing of her upset daughter.

"It's my turn to bring cookies for Cubbies tonight? Thanks for reminding me," she says and hangs up the phone. Sighing, she hopelessly looks at the unwashed dishes stacked in the sink as the baby in the next room joins in the chorus with her sister.

Did someone say stress? We all experience it in one way or another. God didn't promise us a rose garden, but what did He promise?

1. What is the promise in Hebrews 13:5?

2. God showed His care of individuals in the case of Adam and Eve and Noah. Can you name other people in the Bible to whom God showed His care?

This young mother is having a bad day that just keeps going. Nights run into each other as one child or another has needs. Lack of sleep and too many demands are raising her stress to a level of overwhelming proportions.

God Is Faithful

Elaine may be tempted to walk out the door and keep walking. She is a believer; she does not doubt that she's a child of God. But right this minute she's not sure if that knowledge is enough to get her through the day.

First Corinthians 10:13 contains a promise for times of confusion: "There hath no temptation taken you but such as is common to man: but God is faithful, who will not suffer you to be tempted above that ye are able; but will with the temptation also make a way to escape, that ye may be able to bear it."

3. What does "able to bear" mean?

Elaine picked up her son, Bobby, from school and baked cookies while working with Bobby on his verses for Awana. She washed the dishes, cooked dinner, changed the baby several times, and refereed arguments between siblings. Her husband, a youth pastor, dashes in at 5:30, looking for dinner. He needs to be at church by 6:00 for youth group.

He looks into the pot. "Is this what we're having?" he asks unhappily. "It looks awful." Then he looks around and says, "Look at this place; it's a mess. What have you been doing all day?" He grabs a handful of cookies and leaves for church.

Elaine looks mournfully at the door, then turns and starts

the laborious process of getting everything ready for church. She bundles the kids into the car. Upon her arrival at church, she deposits the children and the cookies in their respective places. She rushes up to the youth meeting where she is in charge of choosing the music and playing the keyboard. She smiles and greets all those she encounters along the way.

To the people she meets, Elaine seems to be happy and in control. She has followed one of the options for handling her emotions. She is stuffing her feelings.

4. What could happen to a person who continues to stuff feelings?

Am I Balanced?

Elaine needs to stop and evaluate her stress level. She is tired, hurt, and angry. Everyone wants to be her top priority, and she is trying to please all of them. Can she juggle everything and still maintain spiritual and emotional balance?

God designed our bodies, souls, and spirits to work together in balance. Sometimes we discover that our emotions have tipped the scale, and we find ourselves totally out of balance.

5. How can we tell when we are out of balance?

6. What should we do if our life is out of balance?

The psalmist requested of God, "Lead me in the way everlasting" (Psalm 139:24). To discover where we are out of balance, we need to go to the One Who created us.

We are the only ones who can examine ourselves to see if anger, bitterness, or jealousy is present. Proverbs 14:10 tells us, "The heart knoweth his own bitterness."

Pain is personal. We have private issues that we don't share with others. At times we don't even know ourselves where the source of our pain lies. Only God knows what is in the depths of our hearts. "Search me, O God, and know my heart: try me, and know my thoughts: and see if there be any wicked way in me, and lead me in the way everlasting" (Psalm 139:23, 24).

We may lie to ourselves to cover pain. It is easier to call those lies "rationalization." If we refuse to address a painful situation long enough, the stress fractures show in other areas, like in our relationships with loved ones.

We must be careful *not* to look to people to meet a need that only God can meet. "My soul, wait thou only upon God; for my expectation is from him" (Psalm 62:5).

Read Psalm 62:6–8.

7. In many of the psalms, David wrote from personal experience about trusting God. Can you think of times when David's trust was tested?

Understanding Our Losses Gives Balance

8. What kind of losses was Elaine suffering?

It is not enough to acknowledge and understand our losses. Sometimes it's necessary to grieve for them.

The Goal of Grieving Our Loss Is Acceptance

Recognizing what upsets us is a step toward dealing with the overwhelming demands on our lives. When we can *accept* the loss, we are ready to move on. Acceptance doesn't mean we are whipped puppies, going on our way with our heads down in despair. Acceptance is, instead, an acknowledgement that God will provide grace to carry on, just as He has promised.

Sharing the Load

Elaine confronted her husband later that evening. She waited until the kids were in bed and there were no pressing distractions. She said, "Honey, I have a problem, and you're the only one who can help me."

She presented the facts in a nonthreatening way. "I know you have a busy schedule, and I appreciate the way you are taking good financial care of us. But you should know that after you came home and complained about the house and the dinner, I felt bad all evening."

John looked at her and, for the first time that evening, considered how his actions had affected her. "I'm sorry, Elaine. I was in such a hurry. I'd been running all day from meeting to meeting. The truth is that I stopped by the house only to grab my books for the youth meeting. I didn't have time to stop and eat."

Elaine explained how those few hurtful words could have long-lasting effects on the children's attitude toward her and their parents' marriage.

John nodded in response, "I know you're right. We need to pray for wisdom in our relationship and that God will open our eyes to the influence we have on our children. If we want our children to learn to walk with the Lord, we need to be role models for them."

9. Read John 8:32. What are some important Biblical truths you can tell yourself in stressful times?

Where Is My Focus?

The things we focus on affect our emotional balance. For instance, if a child breaks a favorite vase, I might shrug my shoulders and say, "Oh well! It's no big deal." Then as the day wears on, I bump into a table, leaving a painful bruise on my leg. The laundry has a pen in it, and all the shirts get ink stains on them. All day long I continue to rehearse what went wrong. Each person I meet hears, "I have had the worst day. It all started when Sally dropped my favorite vase. . . ." It's time to admit it: dropping that vase was a big deal. It hurt to sweep up the precious pieces of glass. I should have stopped right away, acknowledged the loss, put it in perspective, and gone on with the day. I should rehearse in my mind the good things and let go of the painful mishaps.

10. How can our focus affect our attitude?

11. Why should we take time to grieve our losses?

12. Does God care about a broken vase?

Luke 10:38–42 records an incident involving two sisters. Martha was obsessive about her work. She wanted her sister to be obsessive too. But Mary wanted to listen to Jesus. She wasn't being lazy; she just couldn't tear her attention away from what was going on. Martha became angry and complained, "Lord, don't You care that my sister has left me to serve alone? Tell her to help me."

Jesus answered, "Martha, Martha, thou art careful and troubled about many things: But one thing is needful: and Mary hath chosen that good part, which shall not be taken away from her" (vv. 41, 42).

Jesus cared enough about that small argument between sisters that He recorded it in His Word. Other personal incidents in Scripture indicate God's interest in people's daily lives.

Do I Share Too Much?

There is another response to stress that sometimes causes more pain than stuffing does: *dumping* your stressful situations on anyone who will listen. Think carefully about the things you share with others—especially those private disagreements you have with your spouse. Consider Elaine's position as a youth pastor's wife. If Elaine recounts to others the little fractious moments with her husband, her friends in church could "take sides" and adversely affect his ministry. If she has told them about the insulting way John spoke to her at dinner but hasn't been able to share with them how they resolved the situation in a godly way, her friends might continue to carry a grudge, possibly never forgetting the incident.

Think of good things to report to your husband or friends. If your day wasn't spectacular, share a promise you read in Scripture. "Speaking to yourselves in psalms and hymns and spiritual songs, singing and making melody in your heart to the Lord; giving thanks always for all things unto God and the Father in the name of our Lord Jesus Christ" (Ephesians 5:19, 20).

Let your life be exuding the love of God, not covering up a cauldron of repressed emotions.

Kim was coaching the girls' basketball team at the Christian high school. She arrived for choir practice a few minutes late because of an important game. Her team had lost. She was upset but tried to act as though the loss was unimportant. Her friend Donna asked, "Are you okay?"

Kim shrugged her shoulders, "Oh, it's nothing. We lost the game, but it's no big deal."

Donna put her arm around Kim's shoulders. "Kim, losing the game was a big deal to you and the girls. You need to admit it and grieve the loss. If you keep silent about your disappointment and stuff it inside, it will continue to bother you. Face it squarely; then put it behind you. Believe me, it will be better for you and the team. That doesn't mean that you have to run around saying, 'We lost! We lost! Oh! Woe is me.' Just make sure you tell yourself the truth: the game was an important event to you."

13. How did God provide for His servant, Elijah, during a difficult time? Read 1 Kings 17:6.

When we see how God provided for people throughout the Bible, we can be assured that He will provide for us as well.

The Right Focus

14. A great way to keep your focus on the right things is to read Philippians 4:8. What does it suggest we think about?

Things that are _____

Things that are _____

Things that are _____

Things that are _____

Things that are _____

Things that are _____

Things that are _____

Things that are _____

One way to focus on things that are true and praiseworthy is to keep a journal of blessings, including answers to prayers and things for which you are grateful. Keep your journal current, and add to it frequently. Anytime you need a lift, look at your blessings list and focus on what God has done.

Where Does Joy Come From?

Joy does not come from material possessions. Sometimes I hear people say, "If only I had a new house, I'd be happy"; "If only I had a new car, I'd be happy"; or "If only I could go shopping for a new wardrobe, I'd be happy." Houses get messy and need cleaning, the paint peels, and weeds grow in the garden. Cars get scratched. Clothes wear out. And so goes the joy of possessions.

The joy of possessions changes with perspective. If you have a cupboard full of raisins, they don't seem too important. (You might not even like raisins.) But if you are hungry and have only one raisin, that raisin becomes very important.

God's Word can be like that. We have the Bible to read and encourage us, but we don't always take advantage of it. However, in times of stress, the Word takes on a huge new meaning.

Joy does not come from circumstances. In most cases we can't choose our circumstances. Circumstances involve our own health and the health of our loved ones, the places we live, weather conditions, and national disasters. If our joy depended on these events, it would come and go constantly.

15. What is the source of joy? Read Galatians 5:22.

16. How can we maintain joy in our lives in spite of circumstances?

17. Read Colossians 3:1–4. Where should our focus be?

18. Read Jeremiah 9:23 and 24. In what thoughts of ours does God delight?

Maintaining balance is a matter of both completing the tasks God has supplied us the ability to accomplish and placing the unattainable into *His* hands.

Placing our struggles into God's hands is a key to maintaining balance in a stress-filled world.

LESSON 2

In
His Care

THE CALL CAME AS we were leaving the house on a rainy Thursday evening. My husband was urging me to hurry because we would be late for a meeting that he was to chair at church. As I took the phone call, I knew immediately it was more important than a meeting.

My dad's voice came sorrowfully over the line, "Your brother Doug is not doing well. He's not expected to live for more than a few days." I listened in shocked silence as Dad related Doug's final journey. "Doug flew to Denver to visit friends. He looked good when he left, but it just took too much out of him. After the plane landed, the cancer struck the final blow and incapacitated him. He flew home in an ambulance plane. He's come home to die."

I responded the way my father expected: "I'll be there as soon as I can make the reservations."

So many memories flooded my mind as I sat on the plane. Doug had been reared in a Christian home. My mother and father had served the Lord faithfully all their lives. We six children were brought up in church. Getting us ready on Sunday mornings was no small task. We kids wondered why we weren't invited to other people's homes very often. We didn't realize it was a pretty big undertaking to have eight guests over for dinner.

Having a large family didn't stop my mother from playing hostess to anyone who needed a good Sunday dinner. We were blessed to have evangelists and missionaries visit our home on Sunday afternoons. What great role models my parents were! We didn't understand the sacrifices in time and finances they made to be hospitable until we had families of our own.

Why Would God Take Away Someone So Precious?

My brother Doug was everybody's favorite. He was musically talented and fun to be with. He was a genius. As a four-year-old child he had a vocabulary so large that neighbors used to sit on their porches and talk to him just to hear him use big words in context.

At forty-five he was in his last moments of life. What those around him were about to witness was not about death; it was about the meaning of life.

By the time I arrived, Doug had been settled in his home with his twenty-three-year-old daughter, Chelsea. She had taken off from work and college to care for her dad. What a trooper she was, sleeping by his side and responding to his every movement. Even though he couldn't talk, she knew when he wanted a drink or medicine. He couldn't swallow, so any pain medication had to be absorbed in the side of his mouth.

Doug's son, Nathan, also came to be with him. The love of those two dedicated young people was beautiful to see.

My parents and I went to see Doug often over the next few days. As we prepared to leave for another visit, the call came: "Doug just passed away."

We rushed to his house. It was filled with friends. My father fell on Doug's body and mournfully cried—letting out the anguish of the last few days and months. Then we prayed, not for the one who had died, because we knew he was already pain free and in a far better place. We prayed for the living who were experiencing pain almost beyond endurance. And then Doug's friends, all fine musicians, surrounded his body and joined in a heartfelt chorus of "Amazing Grace." The sound will always ring in my memory. God used it to deliver His grace in a time of extreme emotional turmoil.

1. Read John 3:16 and Galatians 2:20. How is God's love described in these two verses?

The death of a loved one brings an intense amount of stress into our lives. During that time, maintaining balance is hard. The things we are sure of—our salvation and God's existence—are not in question, but the depth of despair caused by the pain of missing our loved one can bring any number of emotions. Guilt might rear its ugly head because we didn't take time to visit the sick person. Maybe the last words we shared were spoken in anger. A parent who loses a child may remember only the harsh words he or she spoke right before an accident took that precious child's life.

Anger can become an obsession. Some may ask why God would take such a *good* person when there are so many bad people in the world.

Parents experience a special kind of grief when burying a child. No parents expect to bury their own child. They have always thought that their children would bury them one day.

Depression can follow the death of a loved one. Grieving people may not be interested in going on with life. They feel tired and listless. Entertainment diversions seem inappropriate in the face of their great loss. They withdraw from their friends. Words can't touch their pain.

How Are We Supposed to Get Over Our Grief?

Acknowledging the loss of a loved one is an important part of maintaining emotional balance. To mourn that loss leads to acceptance. But what if we're stuck in the mourning process and can't move on?

2. What instruction do we read in Hebrews 12:15?

My parents went to the proper source for solace. They understood the teachings of Scripture. They were comforted by the promises of the Word. Isaiah 41:10 took on new meaning for them.

3. What does Isaiah 41:10 mean to you?

In times of grief we learn much about the kind of relationship we have with God. Those who have accepted Christ as their Savior experience the solace of the Holy Spirit as He ministers to them. The apostle Paul wrote, "But I would not have you to be ignorant, brethren, concerning them which are asleep, that [you] sorrow not, even as others which have no hope. For if we believe that Jesus died and rose again, even so them also which sleep in Jesus will God bring with him" (1 Thessalonians 4:13, 14).

My parents had the peace of God because of a step they had taken as young people when they realized what Jesus had done for them.

4. Read John 3:16. What is true for each person who "believeth in him"?

5. According to John 10:10, why did Christ come to earth?

6. What separates us from God? Read Romans 3:23.

7. Read Proverbs 14:12. When we try to reach God our own way, what happens?

8. What do the following verses tell us about how to have the abundant life mentioned in John 10:10?

1 Timothy 2:5

1 Peter 3:18

Romans 5:8

John 1:12

Romans 10:9

Acts 16:31

9. How can we have hope in response to tragic events? Read Hebrews 4:16.

King David recorded his trust in God through many hair-raising adventures: "For I have heard the slander of many: fear was on every side: while they took counsel together against me, they devised to take away my life. But I trusted in thee, O LORD: I said, Thou art my God" (Psalm 31:13, 14).

10. Read John 10:27–30. What assurance do we have that God hasn't abandoned us in our despair?

11. Why do we need to trust God when we go through difficult experiences? Read Isaiah 55:8.

12. What comfort does Romans 8:28 give?

13. Both Isaiah 40:31 and Isaiah 41:10 talk about something the Lord gives to those who trust in Him. What is it?

When we are going through the grieving process, it is difficult to focus on the truths we should be telling ourselves. It's easy to rationalize and blame God for our despair, but there is only one source of truth.

14. According to John 14:6, _____ is the truth.

15. Read John 14:2. What promise gives us comfort?

Years ago I attended Western Baptist Bible College in El Cerrito, California. Death seemed like a faraway experience until one day in June. A recent graduate, a beautiful girl who had everything to live for, went to work for a Christian agency in another state. Her name was Carolyn. She had a bubbly personality, and everyone liked being around her. She was called to serve the Lord—but she suddenly died of leukemia at the age of twenty. She didn't even know she had the disease.

A disbelieving crowd stood at the graveside. Doctor H. O. Van Gilder, the college president, delivered the message. I have never forgotten his words: "Don't think of Carolyn as gone, but think of her as if she were on a missionary journey. You would gladly say good-bye, knowing she was off doing the Father's will. That is exactly what she's doing."

Did the words stop the pain of separation? No, but they provided a different perspective on the situation. We could fill our minds with the promises of Scripture, with the joy of seeing the Savior face-to-face: "But as it is written, Eye hath not seen, nor ear heard, neither have entered into the heart of man, the things which God hath prepared for them that love him" (1 Corinthians 2:9).

Dwell on the Promises

The only way to maintain balance during a time of overwhelming grief is to dwell on the promises of God. Grieving has several levels. Sometimes grief doesn't come from a personal loss. It may come from something we see in the news involving death and starvation in our country or others. Focusing on newspaper and television accounts of disaster is enough to discourage anyone. We need to balance the details that bombard our minds with the truths of God's Word.

16. Of what important truths does 2 Corinthians 4:16–18 remind us?
Our affliction, or trouble, is _____.

It works for us _____ that outweighs the affliction, or trouble.

We look at the things that are _____.

The things that are seen are _____.

The unseen things are _____.

17. According to 1 Thessalonians 4:13, what is true of our sorrow?

God has answers. Think of His Word as His news report to us. The more we study the Bible, the more we find the treasures He included for our benefit.

Second Corinthians 4:16 deals with the infirmities of aging: "Though our outward man perish, yet the inward man is renewed day by day." This verse made a fresh impression on me after I attended the funeral of a dear friend. (As my husband and I age, funerals become a far too common occurrence.) In my discouragement I picked up my Bible for devotions, and the promise of 2 Corinthians 4:16 leaped out at me. Even though we are unable to do some of the activities we did years ago, we have the promise that the Holy Spirit will continually renew our inward person. We may be old on the outside, but we're young on the inside.

If we dwell on the truths of the Word, there should be no place for bitterness or resentment when grief comes.

• *Don't* allow rebellion against God to control your life.

• *Don't* allow that "root of bitterness" to spring up.

• *Do* dwell on the promises in God's Word, and be prepared to be used in the service of the Lord.

God has left you here for a purpose. Psalm 31:15 reassures us that our times are in His hands. Make the most of your years!

18. Ephesians 5:15–20 gives us several commands that will help us maintain the proper perspective.

_____, or live, circumspectly, or carefully.

_____, or make the most of, the time.

_____ what the will of the Lord is.

Yielding to the Holy Spirit so we can _____ _____ with, or be controlled by, Him.

_____ to one another with hymns and spiritual songs, making melody in your heart to the Lord.

Always give _____.

19. First Thessalonians 5:14–18 describes things that are the will of the Lord for us.

_____ those who are unruly, or idle.

_____ the feebleminded, or timid.

_____ the weak.

Be _____ to everyone.

Make sure we don't render, or pay back, _____ for

_____.

Follow that which is _____ .

_____ always.

_____ without ceasing.

_____ _____ in everything (all circumstances).

When Martha was mourning the loss of Lazarus, Jesus told her, "I am the resurrection, and the life: he that believeth in me, though he were dead, yet shall he live" (John 11:25). It was not too long after this experience with Lazarus that mourners stood at the foot of the cross in deep sorrow. They had lost all hope, but in just three days their sorrow turned to joy as they learned of Christ's resurrection. And today—because of His resurrection—we can have joy in the midst of sorrow.

How can we maintain balance in a time of intensified emotional stress? God has commanded us to simply trust Him, and He has promised to be our strength in times of trouble: "Come unto me, all ye that labour and are heavy laden, and I will give you rest" (Matthew 11:28).

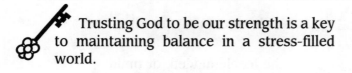 Trusting God to be our strength is a key to maintaining balance in a stress-filled world.

Who Am I, Really?

ELISSA, FILLED WITH excitement, entered the church. The congregation had called a new minister of music; this was Melissa's first chance to see how he conducted the song service. After an absence of two weeks, she was glad to be back. Melissa walked up to the front and took her place at the piano to start the prelude.

The new music director approached and cleared his throat. "I didn't have a chance to contact you this week, but Sandra Martin is going to play on Sunday evenings from now on."

Sandra Martin, Melissa thought, *she's that new woman who's only been in the church a few weeks.*

Embarrassed and shaken, Melissa walked to the back of the church. She was stunned. Turning to her husband, she said tearfully, "I've been replaced." Her thoughts were in such turmoil that she couldn't stay in the service. She went out and sat in the car and tried to understand what was happening.

How could this happen? she thought. *I've been playing here for ten years. I'm always faithful; I'm never late. Sure, I was gone for two weeks, but those were the only Sundays I've missed in all these years. Who does this guy think he is? Why didn't someone tell him that I'm the piano player here? God gave me the gift of music, and He expects me to use it. If they don't do something about this,*

I'm leaving. I'll go to a church that appreciates me. Music is what I am. Without my music ministry, I am nothing.

Are Melissa's feelings true? What lies was Melissa telling herself?

The Bible says, "[You] are not your own . . . [you] are bought with a price" (1 Corinthians 6:19, 20). God called us according to His purpose, not according to our works (2 Timothy 1:9).

Melissa was thinking only of herself. She was quickly traveling through the steps of grieving—disbelief, denial, shock, anger, and depression. The next day painful thoughts pressed in on Melissa. *I'm a has-been,* she told herself.

Her husband's response, "Snap out of it. You're acting like a spoiled child," didn't help.

The sympathy and indignation of friends at the "unfair situation" didn't help either. Those responses fed Melissa's wrong thinking.

Melissa was convinced that no one could understand her pain. She was praying, but she was unwilling to listen to God. She wanted Him to answer her way and to change things back to the way they had been.

The more Melissa brooded over the problem, the worse she felt. She wallowed in self-pity for several days until the music minister called.

"I'm sorry about Sunday evening," he said. "I just learned there was a problem. You were away on vacation, and I assumed Sandra was the main pianist. I didn't mean to hurt your feelings. Please accept my apology. Would you help me work out a schedule so all the musicians can be included in the ministry?"

As Melissa thought about the significance of his call, she realized things would never be the same again. There was no answer to this problem. She knew she didn't want to share the music responsibility. She wanted to do it all herself—her way. If she complained, she would sound like a spoiled child.

Although the music minister had done the appropriate thing, Melissa felt rejected. She didn't care that he had been honest. As far as she was concerned, she had a right to feel sad. It was at this point that Melissa came to the end of herself. Her solutions were only making her unhappier by the minute. Friends couldn't help—they couldn't understand her pain. Where could she turn?

She asked herself, *Is this problem too big for God?* Melissa began to pray. Verses she had learned over the years came to her, washing away the pain in her heart.

1. What could Melissa learn from Philippians 1:20 and 27 and 4:8?

Why Do I Worship?

After she prayed, Melissa began to think about worship. *Why do I go to church? Is it to show off? If I don't have a part of the service, am I going to stay home?*

2. What is your purpose in going to church?

3. Consider Hebrews 10:24 and 25. What reason for worshiping together do these verses give?

4. Is using our talents a good reason to attend church?

5. How does 2 Timothy 1:9 relate to this question?

6. Titus 3:5 states that God saved us because of His _____,

   not because of the righteous _____ we have done.

Our good works cannot save us. Only trusting Christ as our Savior and accepting His gift of eternal life can do that. But after our rebirth, we are commanded to think of others.

Responding to Hurts

7. If someone hurts us, how should we respond?

8. How does Colossians 3:13 help answer this question?

One way to get past depression and hurt is to look for ways to encourage others. Look outside your circle of pity and try to identify others who are hurting. When you help others, your pain will diminish. It is hard to think of others and yourself at the same time. God expects us to accomplish good works in response to His act of love in buying our salvation with the blood of Christ.

9. Second Corinthians 6:1 says, "We then, as workers to-gether with him." Who is "him"? What does this relationship make us?

The Place of Good Works

10. According to Colossians 1:10, we are to live, or walk, _____ of the Lord to please Him. We are also to bear fruit, or be fruitful, in what?

11. Philippians 2:13 reminds us that God _____ in us to will (intend) and to do His good _____.

12. What does Ephesians 2:10 say we are created for?

13. What do you think these "good works" are? (Compare Ephesians 2:10 with Ephesians 2:8 and 9.)

14. List some of the good works that should be part of a Christian's lifestyle.

15. For whom could you do the good work of encouragement?

Each of us has an important place in her church—whether it's teaching Sunday School, singing in the choir, or praying in the pew. No job is *the most* important. Remember that changes will come. Situations change. Health can become a factor in our service. We need to live each moment in the power of the Spirit—to be open to God's leading in every facet of our lives, including our service to Him. Reflect on your position. Does "nursery worker" seem like an unimportant ministry compared to "musician"?

Be content where you are. That is the right place for you today. God has prepared you for His service just as He prepared Jeremiah: "Before I formed thee in the belly I knew thee; and before thou camest forth out of the womb I sanctified thee, and I ordained thee a prophet unto the nations" (Jeremiah 1:5).

Reading the truths in God's Word helped Melissa achieve the balance she needed. After rehearsing in her mind the good things God had done, she recognized her need to take stock of her spiritual condition. She admitted to herself that her whole life didn't revolve around music. She faced the truth that she didn't comprise all the musical talent in the church. God had given her talent, and He had the right to direct its use.

16. Read 2 Corinthians 10:5. How can we obey this command?

Melissa needed to consider others (Hebrews 10:24). Sandra also has musical talent. How would Melissa's selfish refusal to allow Sandra to take part in the music ministry affect Sandra?

Looking at the situation from a balanced perspective, Melissa came to realize things would not go back to the way they used to be. She is glad. Worship is more meaningful to her now. Taking turns at playing for services has given a refreshing break from responsibility. Now Melissa has more time to focus on the real meaning of worship.

Our talents can be used for God only when we place them in His hands to do with as He pleases. No woman is just a wife, a mother, or a grandmother. These roles can describe us, but in the fiber of our being, each of us believers is God's child.

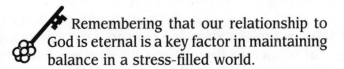

Remembering that our relationship to God is eternal is a key factor in maintaining balance in a stress-filled world.

I Don't Want to Be Like That

WHAT'S THE MATTER, Julie?" Ann asked.

"Oh, it's my mother," Julie replied. "She came for a visit, and I wasn't sure I'd make it through the week. She's such a gossip, and she complains so much. Every time I'm with her, I get depressed. Sometimes I sound just like her, and I don't want to be like that. What can I do?"

Ann patted Julie's shoulder, "Let's see what God's Word has to say about your problem. Even though we wish we could be different, we aren't capable of changing ourselves. Only the One Who created us has the power to change us. Romans 12:2 says, 'Be not conformed to this world: but be ye transformed by the renewing of your mind, that ye may prove what is that good, and acceptable, and perfect, will of God.' We can't renew our own minds, but God can," stated Ann.

Julie shrugged her shoulders. "What you're saying makes sense, but where do I start?"

Ann laughed, "You've already started. Realizing there's a problem is the first step, and looking to the right source for the answer is the correct response."

Julie asked, "Is a little gossip such a bad thing? I don't think my mother sees it as a sin."

Ann pointed to her Bible. "James 3:5 says, 'Even so the tongue is a little member, and boasteth great things. Behold, how great a matter a little fire kindleth!' James 3:7 and 8 go on to say that animals can be tamed by man but that no one can tame the tongue. It is evil and full of deadly poison. That doesn't sound too innocent."

"How can I get my mom to quit gossiping?" Julie asked.

"You can't. We can be responsible only for our own actions, but you might be able to channel the discussion into something more positive. You could say, 'Can we talk about something else, Mom? I'm uncomfortable talking about someone who isn't here to defend herself. Maybe what you've heard isn't the whole story.' "

Julie smiled. "That might work. I'll try it."

"One thing to remember—it's not our business to change lives; it's God's business. Our responsibility is to pray for others and leave the results in His hands. When we identify a fault in our own lives, we have the obligation to target that fault with our prayers for change. God never asks anyone to do anything that He doesn't provide the ability to accomplish."

"I have one other suggestion," Ann said. "When a conversation turns toward something negative, try to counter with a positive statement. For instance, if someone brings up a common acquaintance, 'Did you hear about Jane? She's so bitter about her sister's award,' you could say, 'I don't see how that can be, she's so talented herself.' Injecting a positive note into the conversation will direct it away from gossip."

Ann continued, "In fact, I've seen a woman, ready to go for the kill on some story she had heard, become speechless in response to a dose of truth. But the idea is not to show one-upmanship. It's to show God's love."

Julie replied, "Thank you, Ann, for sharing these important truths with me. I think with a little planning ahead, I can make my next visit with Mom more pleasant. Sometimes I wish she were more like Amanda Jones. She's so sweet. I've never heard her say anything derogatory about anyone. When I'm a senior citizen, that's how I want to be."

"That's another positive thing you can do to age gracefully. Select older women who are spiritually mature. Use them for your role models. Write down the qualities that make them stand out as virtuous women; then strive to incorporate those qualities into your life. In addition, you can reflect on the good qualities of your mother. Make a list of them and the things she does that you are grateful for. If you're stuck for a positive comment in conversation, tell her you appreciate her for _____. Fill in the blank with items from your list. It could change your relationship with your mother. Commit each day to the Lord. Ask God to search your heart and control your conversation. No person can control the tongue [James 3:8]. Man can't, but God can."

1. What kind of life has God called us to live (1 Thessalonians 4:7)? What can we find in our time of need (Hebrews 4:16)?

2. What traits have you noticed in mature Christian women that you would like to imitate?

3. Titus 2:3–5 includes a list of things we can learn from mature women in the church. What are they?

4. Read Colossians 3:8–17. According to verse 10, we are to put on the _____ man. In Whose image is she being renewed?

5. According to Colossians 2:6 and 7, we should walk by faith and abound with what trait?

6. Read Colossians 4:6. How should our speech be characterized?

7. Read Ephesians 4:29 and then summarize what our conversation should be like. Why do you think it should be like that?

8. What do our words reveal about us? How can our speech bring honor or dishonor to the Lord?

9. Read Philippians 1:20. Why did Paul weigh his words so carefully?

10. How can we prepare ourselves to converse in a godly manner? (See Ephesians 6:11–18.)

11. Does "speaking the truth in love" (Ephesians 4:15) mean "being brutally honest"? What does it mean?

12. James said no man could tame the tongue (James 3:8), and most of us have probably found that to be true. So how can we have victory in this area of our speech? Read Ephesians 4:20–32 and jot down some practical suggestions.

13. What does 2 Corinthians 5:10 tell us about who is responsible for our actions?

14. How can 1 Corinthians 10:13 help you if you are caught in a conversation featuring gossip and slander? What "escapes" can you use?

15. David kept a balanced perspective in his conversation. According to Psalm 19:14, what did he focus on?

Julie is on the way to having a better relationship with her mother. She is learning ways to guide conversation in a more God-honoring direction without embarrassing her mother. In addition, Julie has gained a new appreciation for the qualities of her mother that Julie admired as a child. Her mother is blooming under the display of gratitude from her daughter. Envy and bitterness that caused her to gossip have given way to other avenues of conversation.

Begin today to make David's prayer your daily request of the Lord: "Let the words of my mouth, and the meditation of my heart, be acceptable in thy sight, O LORD, my strength, and my redeemer" (Psalm 19:14).

Understanding that our words are an extension of our thoughts is important. Guarding our thoughts and words is a job we cannot handle ourselves. Help is available!

Asking God to guard our hearts, minds, and tongues is an important key to maintaining balance in a stress-filled world.

The
Gift
of Pain

THE LITTLE BOY stretched his hand toward the flame. As the fire licked his fingers, he didn't withdraw. The child smiled at the pretty plaything until he was snatched from the "toy" by his frantic mother.

What was the child's problem? He was born with a rare condition that prevented his pain receptors from telling his brain that his body was in danger. The signal of pain was missing from his life.

When Ron was injured in an accident, he became a paraplegic. He had no feeling below his waist. One day Ron sat too close to an electric heater. He wasn't aware of the fire until a friend shouted that his pants were burning. The doctors treated the severe burn on Ron's leg without anesthetic. How could this happen? Ron didn't feel the pain.

Pain is vital. It keeps us from destroying ourselves. Someone has described pain as "the gift nobody wants."

Pain in our physical bodies indicates danger. The same is true in our spiritual life: emotional pain is a warning. It's important for us to recognize the cause of our pain, for identifying the problem is the first step toward finding a remedy.

God can do more with a broken woman than He can with a woman who thinks she can run everything her own way. A person who knows she cannot master pain must rely on God to see her through.

David was a broken man after committing adultery and, to cover his sin, arranging the murder of a courageous man (2 Samuel 11). He turned to God for forgiveness and comfort (2 Samuel 12).

1. When David acknowledged his sin, how did Nathan respond (2 Samuel 12:13)?

2. David confessed his sin and was forgiven. But what pain did he suffer as a consequence of his sin (2 Samuel 12:14–23)?

God used David in a great way after he confessed his sin. He became the most beloved king of Israel. God promised David that one of his descendents would be the Messiah. His son Solomon became the richest king in history. God blessed David's life because David humbled himself and repented of his sin.

3. What did David write about God in Psalm 103:10 and 11?

4. Why does God allow trials into our lives (2 Corinthians 1:8, 9)?

Paul focused on the *benefits* of pain rather than on the *difficulty* of the pain.

5. Do our actions cause our pain? Explain your answer.

6. List some things that cause us pain.

Many times the pain in our lives comes from external sources. Consider the life of Joseph (Genesis 37—50). If anyone had an excuse to be bitter, it was Joseph. His jealous brothers sold him into slavery. Then a spiteful woman wrongfully accused him. While in jail, he rose to the highest position in the prison. There he correctly interpreted the dreams of two fellow prisoners. One man, a butler, returned to his position in Pharaoh's court—as Joseph had predicted. But the butler forgot to tell Pharaoh about Joseph as he had promised. Two years passed before the butler remembered Joseph.

7. What does Genesis 39:21 record about this time in Joseph's life?

8. How did Joseph react to the pain in his life? Read Genesis 40:6 and 7 and 50:20.

Had Joseph not been sent to prison, he probably would not have met the butler. He was brought before Pharaoh to interpret a dream and ultimately became the second highest ruler in the land of Egypt, the greatest kingdom on earth at the time. With God's guidance, Joseph saved the world from famine and preserved the Hebrew people.

Joseph maintained spiritual balance during his years as a prisoner. He put painful memories aside when he spoke to his brothers. Joseph was the ruler when his brothers came to beg for food. They bowed down to him and asked him for a favor. Some people would have relished this opportunity to reprimand the brothers for what they had done years before. But Joseph did not harbor anger. He said, "Fear not: for am I in the place of God? But as for you, ye thought evil against me; but God meant it unto good, to bring to pass, as it is this day, to save much people alive" (Genesis 50:19, 20).

If Joseph had not experienced the great pain of separation, he would have grown up in the house of Jacob far from Egypt. The world—and possibly his family—would have starved. Because God allowed Joseph to go through painful situations, all history has been affected by his life.

Pressure to Precious

Earth's pressure can turn dirt into diamonds. Pearls are produced because of an irritating piece of sand. As we submit to God, our pain, caused by pressure and irritations, can produce diamonds and pearls in our lives.

9. Jot down a time when God used pain in your life to give you spiritual insight.

Can we say with the psalmist, "But it is good for me to draw near to God: I have put my trust in the Lord GOD, that I may declare all thy works" (Psalm 73:28)?

10. What practical things can we do during times of pain?

King David, the man after God's own heart (Acts 13:22), set the example of how we should respond to pain: "I cried unto God with my voice, even unto God with my voice; and he gave ear unto me. In the day of trouble I sought the Lord" (Psalm 77:1, 2).

Meditate on these other helpful Scripture passages:

"Casting all your care upon him; for he careth for you" (1 Peter 5:7).

"Humble yourselves in the sight of the Lord, and he shall lift you up" (James 4:10).

"Let us therefore come boldly unto the throne of grace, that we may obtain mercy, and find grace to help in time of need" (Hebrews 4:16).

Consider Paul, who started out as Saul, persecuting the church. After meeting the Lord on the road to Damascus, he suffered the pain of blindness (Acts 9:3–9). Then he suffered the pain of rejection as the leaders of the church were afraid of him (Acts 9:26). Some questioned his salvation. He was beaten and imprisoned because of his faith (2 Corinthians 11:23–28). God allowed these things in his life, and he became the greatest missionary the world has ever known.

Paul was a man of great spiritual balance. He said, "I am the least of the apostles, that am not meet to be called an apostle, because I persecuted the church of God. But by the grace of God I am what I am: and his grace which was bestowed upon me was not in vain; but I laboured more abundantly than they all: yet not I, but the grace of God which was with me" (1 Corinthians 15:9, 10).

The human heart tends to run from pain. We don't want to acknowledge its existence. We fight against pain, hoping it will go away. If we deny the pain, we won't have to respond. Denial can lead to depression. But to "embrace your pain" means to accept it and learn from it.

Better or Bitter?

11. How can we maintain a proper balance in spite of our pain?

If our pain involves our need for forgiveness, we must ask God to search our hearts: "Search me, O God, and know my heart: try me, and know my thoughts" (Psalm 139:23). God graciously forgives our sins. We must be willing to follow that example and forgive others for the pain they inflict on us.

Psalm 51 records David's plea to God for forgiveness after his terrible sin with Bathsheba. Many times a believer must repeat the words, "Create in me a clean heart, O God; and renew a right spirit within me" (Psalm 51:10).

Forgiveness is God's solution for a bitter heart. Think about these important truths concerning forgiveness.

Forgiveness is not the same as forgetting.

Our healing begins with our acknowledgement of bitterness.

Remember that forgiveness is a personal choice.

Go to the Lord. Forgiveness is an issue between Him and us.

In order to forgive, we must focus on our own accountability.

Very simply, forgiveness frees us to go on regardless of the response of the other person.

Effective forgiveness does *not* mean we must pretend that our hearts have not been wounded or that what was done to us was okay.

Negative thoughts are counterproductive.

Essentially, focus on the benefits of pain. Your new focus will give a new perspective.

Since our interpretation of a difficult event causes either a positive or a negative response, it is not so much what happens to us but what we tell ourselves about it that matters.

Spiritual growth is one of the benefits of forgiveness.

12. When we experience pain, why do we often choose to withdraw?

13. Why does God allow us to have pain? Read John 9:1–3 and formulate your answer from Jesus' response to the disciples.

Thankful for Pain

To put the subject of pain in perspective, we must look at Christ. He suffered more than anyone else on earth. He suffered rejection, for people didn't believe He was the Messiah (John 1:11). The very ones He came to save wanted Him put to death. The created wanted to destroy the Creator. Could anything be more unbalanced than that?

Christ bore the ultimate pain when He, the righteous Son of God, took our sin on Himself (1 Peter 2:21–24). We humans cannot fathom the injustice of this experience. Nevertheless, Christ came to seek and to save the lost (Luke 19:10). Christ didn't focus on the pain He was enduring; He focused on the people He loved and wanted to help.

14. In Psalm 55:4 David wrote about his pain. Look at verse 22 to discover how he responded to the pain. What is the command and the promise in that verse?

15. What promise did Jesus make in Matthew 11:28?

Considering the pain Christ endured makes our day-to-day irritations seem trite. We are so petty that we wallow in self-pity when someone cuts in line at the supermarket. It's time to put things into proper perspective. We should commit to asking God to give us the spiritual balance we so desperately need.

Sometimes it seems as though our pain—whether physical or emotional—will never end. At times physical pain can cloud our thinking and push all other thoughts from our minds. We may forget that our sovereign, loving God is in control. Concerning emotional pain, some painful situations, such as unresolved conflict with a loved one who has passed away, seemingly have no answer. These burdens of the heart can linger, but praise God, they're not the end. We are not left hopeless. Restitution will take place someday.

"And God shall wipe away all tears from their eyes; and there shall be no more death, neither sorrow, nor crying, neither shall there be any more pain: for the former things are passed away. And he that sat upon the throne said, Behold, I make all things new. And he said unto me, Write: for these words are true and faithful" (Revelation 21:4, 5).

Knowing that our hope is in Christ is a key to maintaining balance in a stress-filled world.

LESSON 6

Is He Listening?

SHE WAS MY BEST friend. We did everything together. Well, almost everything. I was raised in a Christian home, and my friend Charlotte didn't go to church. I didn't want to offend her, so I never talked about religious things. Now as I look back, I wonder if I was too embarrassed to share my faith with her, even though I knew she might never hear about salvation.

After we graduated from high school in California, I went on to Bible college. As I listened to the speakers in chapel and in church on Sundays, the Lord began convicting me of all the missed opportunities to witness to my friends when we were in high school. But what could I do about it now?

When I was home on vacation, our schedules kept Charlotte and me from spending time together. I kept putting off the big discussion I knew we should have.

A year later I married a wonderful Christian man, and we moved to Washington State. As time passed and my relationship with God grew, the concern over my unsaved friend grew too. Feeling that I had to do something to salve my conscience, I wrote a letter of apology to her. I expressed my deep sorrow for not sharing the plan of salvation with her, and I explained how she could be saved.

Finally I could get on with my life. It felt great to do what I should have done years earlier. I just had to wait for her to answer my letter; I was confident that she would accept the Lord, and that was that. I had done my Christian duty.

Two weeks later the letter came back marked, "No one by that name lives at this address." There was no forwarding address.

I waited too long, was all I could think. What now? The situation was totally out of my control.

When situations like this one happen, our only resource is prayer. I began praying earnestly for my friend that day.

Ten years later my husband, three children, and I drove down to California to see Grandma and Grandpa. My mother taught a ladies' Bible study. For years she had been telling me what a great class she had. She asked if I would like to attend the annual luncheon with her. It was a good opportunity to spend the afternoon with my mom, so I was happy to go. After the lunch was served, the mistress of ceremonies asked for testimonies of those ladies who had been saved through the ministry of this Bible study program. The first lady to stand and speak took my breath away. I turned to my mother and asked, "Mom, do you know who that is?"

"Of course," she replied; "she's the daughter of one of the ladies in my group."

"But Mom, that's Charlotte. I've been praying for her for ten years. And did you hear her? She just said she was saved because a Christian neighbor came over and witnessed to her. That's what I've been praying for."

I was overwhelmed with praise to the Lord—not only for Charlotte's salvation, but also because He had allowed me to see how He had answered my prayer.

Charlotte and I got together after the luncheon and caught up on all that had happened since high school. It was a reunion I had never dreamed possible. Some people might say that our meeting again was a strange coincidence, but I believe it was an invaluable lesson on the power of prayer.

1. What are some examples of answered prayer in Scripture?

2. Does God always give us what we ask for in our prayers? Explain your answer.

3. Read Acts 12:1–17. Did Rhoda understand that Peter was the man at the door?

4. Why did the others in the house think Rhoda was crazy?

5. Would it have been easier to believe that an angel, instead of Peter, stood at the door?

6. What did Peter tell the prayer group to do (verse 17)?

7. How do you think this event strengthened the faith of the believers?

8. Give an example or two of answered prayer in your life.

9. Paul wrote that we should "pray without ceasing" (1 Thessalonians 5:17). How can we do that?

10. According to Hebrews 4:16, why should we "come boldly unto the throne of grace"?

Ask a young child what prayer is, and he will tell you, "talking to God." It's as simple as that. And the Bible includes many examples of people who prayed: Abraham, David, Daniel, Job, Elisha, Paul. The most important example is Jesus Christ Himself. He spent many hours of His earthly ministry in prayer. Some of His prayers are recorded in the Gospels.

11. Mark 1:35 tells something of Christ's daily life. How did He begin a new day?

When crowds pressed around the Lord and His ministry day was full, He knew how to handle the stress. Luke 5:16 states, "And he withdrew himself into the wilderness, and prayed."

12. In Luke 22:32 what was Christ's prayer for Peter?

Matthew 26:36–46 records Christ's prayer the night before His arrest. When He checked on His disciples, He found them sleeping. He woke them and asked why they couldn't pray with Him for one hour.

13. Why did Christ tell His disciples to watch and pray (Matthew 26:41)?

14. Mark 14:36 records that Christ prayed, "Abba, Father, all things are possible unto thee; take away this cup from me: nevertheless not what I will, but what thou wilt." How did God answer this prayer?

15. Read James 5:16. What does this verse say about prayer?

16. What happened when Elijah prayed (James 5:17, 18)?

17. What should we do when our prayers are not answered the way we think they should be? Read Proverbs 3:5 and 6.

When our children ask for candy, ice cream, and soft drinks for every meal, we don't give them what they want. Why? Is it because we're not listening? Is it because we don't love them? No! It's because we *do* love them. We want them to eat a balanced diet so they will grow strong and be healthy. So it is with our Heavenly Father. He's listening. He gives us what is good for us, even though it may not be what we asked for.

The disciples watched Christ pray. They wanted to follow His example, but they didn't know how.

18. Read Luke 11:1–4. List some features of the prayer that we commonly call "The Lord's Prayer."

Christ often prayed alone, away from distraction, as the world slept. A mother of three young children doesn't have the opportunity to go somewhere alone for a private time with the Lord. She must snatch a moment here and there. To maintain balance, the busy mom must use her creativity.

Tuck a prayer list in with your shopping list. Then instead of fuming at the long lines in the supermarket, you can pray while you wait. Look for those moments when you are in the shower or when you are on hold on the phone for what seems like hours.

One new mother uses the early morning nursing times for prayer. If you search for moments to pray, you'll find your attitude will improve, and the prayer minutes will add up.

I've spent many hours on the freeway, praying as I drive—which brings up another point. It is not necessary to close your eyes to commune with God. Closing our eyes and bowing our heads is a good way to shut out the world, but it isn't a prerequisite for praying. To "pray without ceasing" is to be in constant communication with God—wherever and whenever we desire.

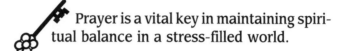 Prayer is a vital key in maintaining spiritual balance in a stress-filled world.

Kept in the Palm of His Hand

THE VALLEY WAS WIDE and deep. I wasn't strong enough to climb out by myself. Mentally I was as far from God as I could get. Even though I was a Christian, my heart was rebellious. I had just lost a job that I loved in a Christian organization. I needed a job, but I was fed up with "Christians and their phony ways." It was time to find a job in the real world where I wouldn't have Christians looking over my shoulder, expecting perfection.

A friend gave me the name of a Christian man who owned a small business and needed a bookkeeper. "No thank you," I said. "I'm not going to work for a Christian."

I planned to get a job on my own. First I interviewed for a secretarial position in a law office. The interview was going great until the lawyer mentioned that he was the attorney for the state lottery. My heart dropped.

"Given your background in Bible college and church affiliation," he asked, "would you have a problem working with the lottery?"

My answer had to be yes.

After I left his office, I began thinking about the piece of paper in my pocket with the Christian businessman's name on it. In my rebellion I hadn't given any thought to what kind of things I might face in the non-Christian workforce, but now I had to face reality. I decided to stop by and check out the available position.

From the moment I entered the shop, I could tell that all the employees were Christians. I had seen some of them at the Christian school my children attended. I asked for an application, and the boss came out and talked to me. He was so enthusiastic about my taking the job that I was intimidated. I tried to tell him I wasn't sure I could do it, but he insisted he could train me. I was relieved to get away. Before I left, he said, "You pray about it, and I'll pray about it; if this is where the Lord wants you, it will work out."

On the way home I thought, *I don't want to pray about it. What if that's where the Lord wants me, but I don't want to be there?*

The next day the shop owner called and asked, "Have you thought about the job?"

"I don't think I'm right for the job," I told him.

He didn't seem to hear my objections. He said, "Come on in. I'll have the bookkeeper show you what you would be doing. I think you should give it a try."

I went in cautiously and was told the job was mine. I agreed to accept on a temporary basis. *I'll try it for a while, and if I don't like it, I'll quit,* I thought.

The boss was good with the customers, and I noticed right away that he witnessed easily to everyone he talked to. It wasn't long before I started feeling secure in the Christian environment. The Lord worked in my heart through the testimony of those around me. As the hardness in my heart melted, so did my skeptical attitude. I recommitted my life to Christ and was able to see that God cared for me and protected me in spite of myself.

After I'd worked for that company for two years, the Lord opened the door for me to serve Him in the job of my dreams. I had gone full circle. The Lord drew me back to Himself in a kind, loving way. He didn't allow me to enter an environment that would harm me. He placed me in a position where I was nurtured and loved.

I've often thought of how my life would have been if I had gone my own way. I learned an important lesson: God keeps us in the palm of His hand.

John 10:27 and 28 state, "My sheep hear my voice, and I know them, and they follow me: And I give unto them eternal life; and they shall never perish, neither shall any man pluck them out of my Father's hand."

It's not God's plan for all Christians to work in a Christian environment, but that was His plan for my life. He knew I was spiritually vulnerable, and He knew exactly what I needed to get my life back on the right track. God had mercy on me and protected me from myself until I was strong enough to climb out of the valley of despair.

Am I sorry that God allowed me to walk through the valley of despair? The answer is a resounding *no!* I am a better person for having been through the valley—not because of anything I have done, but because of the realization that God cared for me and lifted me up to the mountaintop where He was waiting with open arms. If there had been no valley, there would have been no mountaintop.

1. Where is God when we are in the valley? Read Hebrews 13:5.

Looking back I can see God's intervention in my life. I learned of dear Christian friends who had been praying for me, and I'm thankful that God answered their prayers.

2. Jonah experienced the ultimate in dark valleys. How did he get there? Read Jonah 1:1–3.

3. How does our being in rebellion against God affect those around us (Jonah 1:4, 5)?

4. Jonah's selfish act of disobedience put the entire ship in jeopardy. What happened when Jonah took responsibility for his actions (Jonah 1:12–15)?

5. How do we know God did not abandon His rebellious prophet (Jonah 1:4)?

Our actions can sometimes cause pain to those we love the most. It seems that the pain is not ever going to go away—even when we acknowledge our sinful actions and follow God's plan of accountability. When we feel that way, we can be plunged further into the depths of despair. That is what happened to Jonah. He knew he was the guilty one. "Throw me overboard to save yourselves," he said. They did, and the storm went away. But Jonah was worse off than he had ever been.

6. How did God show His love for Jonah (Jonah 1:17)?

7. What was Jonah doing while he was in the belly of the large fish (Jonah 2:1)?

8. How did God rescue Jonah (Jonah 2:10)?

God gave Jonah a second opportunity to obey Him. This time Jonah obeyed (Jonah 3:1–3). He could have taken the right ship the first time around and gone the easy way, but he wanted to do things his way.

9. What happens when we try to do things our way?

God has provided many lessons in the Bible to teach us the way to avoid stress in our lives. Many times we don't see the significance of these lessons until we have already fallen victim to our sinful nature.

Read Luke 15:11–24. The Prodigal Son had it all—a loving, rich father who provided all his needs. But these blessings weren't enough for him; he wanted to experience life. So he took his money and left.

He spent all his money and ended up sleeping with the pigs and eating their food. "What have I done?" he asked himself. Luke 15:17 tells us that "when he came to himself, he said, How many hired servants of my father's have bread enough and to spare, and I perish with hunger!"

10. What will it take for you "to come to [yourself]" and appreciate what God has provided for you, His child?

11. What provisions in our spiritual life are similar to those the Prodigal Son enjoyed at home?

12. What did the father do while his son was away (Luke 15:20)?

The story of the Prodigal Son was a parable (an earthly story with a heavenly meaning) told by Christ. It pictures our relationship to God. He offers us riches untold. Our first impulse is to grab them and run to do our own thing in our own way. We struggle until we come to the end of ourselves and realize that without God we can accomplish nothing.

If we stray from God and spend time in a spiritual valley, we must take some steps to regain our spiritual balance. First we must take the action described in 1 John 1:9—we must confess our sin to God. In the process of regaining spiritual balance, we need to make right any wrongs we've done to others. Our families suffer most when we are spiritually unbalanced. To begin the healing, we may have to ask their forgiveness. Beyond our immediate families, we need to determine if we have wronged friends, members of our church family, or other people as well.

13. What are some other steps we can take to regain spiritual balance?

14. After God has lifted us out of the valley, how can we avoid going back? Read the following verses and jot down a strategy from each one.

    Philippians 3:13

Psalm 103:2

Psalm 5:3

1 Thessalonias 5:18

Philippians 4:8

No valley is too steep for the Father's loving arms. If you're struggling, don't wait until a big fish is circling the boat or you're eating with the pigs. The Father is waiting with open arms for you today.

Working through my own dark valley has caused me to be more sensitive to others who are hurting. I am able to say with confidence that the Lord is the answer. He does have a plan, and He cares about each of us no matter the circumstance.

Remembering that we are kept in the palm of God's hand is another key to maintaining spiritual balance.

Bad News, Good News

A BUSINESSMAN MISSED THE boat. He was angry. His frustration turned to elation a few days later. The ship that sailed without him was the *Titanic*.

We often look at missed opportunities as disasters, thinking about what might have been. However, God blesses us in ways we never imagined, opening doors we would not have seen if we had followed our dreams instead of God's plan.

God allows disappointments and roadblocks in our lives to stretch us and help us grow. It's easy to trust God when everything is going our way. But under those circumstances, we tend to ignore Him and focus on ourselves. It's in times of stress that we turn to the Creator for solace and guidance.

I have heard speakers say, "There are no accidents, only incidents." That expression is easier to say when you're not in the middle of a crisis.

It's difficult to face life when we're plagued by "if only."

"If only I had done something different."

"If only we hadn't given Johnny a bicycle for his birthday, he wouldn't have been riding in the street when that car hit him."

"If only I had checked on the baby a few minutes earlier, she might be alive now."

"If only I had gone to the hospital to see Dad before he passed away."

On our darkest days we can't see how anything good could come from our circumstances. But God is the author of happy endings.

Consider the Biblical character Naomi. She was widowed and lost her two sons. She was alone in a land of strangers. She had two daughters-in-law, but with the death of her sons, all hope of grandchildren was gone.

Naomi decided to return to her own country. Her circumstances were so bleak she told people to call her Mara, which means "bitter." It seemed as though life had passed her by.

1. Why was Naomi bitter (Ruth 1:1–6, 20, 21)?

2. What choice did Naomi offer her daughters-in-law (Ruth 1:8)?

3. How did Ruth show her loyalty to Naomi (Ruth 1:16, 17)?

When Naomi and Ruth reached Bethlehem, the town buzzed with questions about them (Ruth 1:19). The timing was significant: it was the beginning of the barley harvest.

Ruth was willing to work for food, so Naomi directed her to a nearby field to pick up grain and corn that had been left behind by the harvesters.

4. Why was Naomi happy when she learned that Ruth had gleaned in the field owned by Boaz (Ruth 2:1)?

5. What did Boaz do to indicate that he noticed Ruth (Ruth 2:5–9, 14–16)?

6. Why did Boaz appreciate Ruth before he was acquainted with her (Ruth 2:11, 12)?

7. Naomi arranged for a special meeting between Ruth and Boaz (Ruth 3:1–4). How did Boaz react when he found Ruth sleeping at his feet (Ruth 3:10–14)?

8. Why could the other kinsman not redeem Naomi's property (Ruth 4:5, 6)?

9. Ruth became one of the most famous great-grandmothers in history. Who was her great-grandson (Ruth 4:17, 21, 22)?

God had not deserted Naomi. He had provided a better life than she could have imagined. Her life was filled with love and joy.

10. How was Naomi blessed (Ruth 4:13–17)?

If grief in your life has caused you to become bitter, read again the story of Naomi. God worked through other people to turn Naomi's grief into gladness.

11. If God has brought you through a time of grief, what or who did He use to minister to you?

Ruth's loyalty and love helped Naomi. Are you willing to allow God to use you to help someone who is grieving?

12. What are some things you can do to minister to someone who is grieving?

13. List some Bible verses that have helped you or other people you know during times of sorrow.

14. Ruth gave up her family and her country to go with Naomi. How was she rewarded for the sacrifice she made for Naomi's sake?

15. Do you have a problem that seems too big for God? Read Matthew 19:26; Mark 10:27; and Luke 1:37 and 18:27. What truth do these verses emphasize?

16. What does Hebrews 3:12 warn us about?

Let there be no doubts in the mind of the believer: God is in control. He is not indifferent to your situation. You can trust Him for the outcome. Do you need to let go of some things in your life and put them into God's hands?

Naomi went from bitter to blessed. It was a rough road, but God didn't desert her. He was there all the time—going before her—preparing the way.

Ruth looked beyond herself. Her thoughts were centered on how she could help Naomi deal with her grief. Do you think it was easy? Remember Ruth was dealing with her own grief at the loss of her husband. She was probably frightened of how she would be treated in a foreign land, but she didn't let that fear stop her. God blessed Ruth for having the courage to follow through with her commitment.

Life is filled with what-ifs. What if Naomi had not returned to Israel? She would have died a bitter, lonely woman. What if Ruth had not followed Naomi? She would never have met Boaz; there would be no King David.

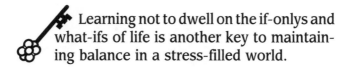 Learning not to dwell on the if-onlys and what-ifs of life is another key to maintaining balance in a stress-filled world.

Serendipity

THE MAN SAT AT the table with the appraiser. He had an apologetic look on his face as he pointed to the object he had brought. "It's just an old ugly picture I found in the attic. I know it's not worth anything, but I thought the frame might be valuable."

The appraiser looked at the item for a few minutes and then called over another dealer to take a look. Finally he turned to the owner and cleared his throat. "I think you'll be surprised at the value of this piece of fabric. The frame is not valuable, but the sampler is worth somewhere in the neighborhood of forty thousand dollars."

The man was aghast. "Are you sure?" he laughed, shaking his head. "I was going to throw it away and keep the frame. It still looks ugly to me."

This man was experiencing serendipity, which according to Webster's dictionary means "the gift of finding valuable or agreeable things not sought for."

In our society serendipity happens frequently. It is one of the things that feeds the garage-sale frenzy—the hope that we can find something valuable for a quarter.

Not long ago I was digging through a junk box at a garage sale and found a ring. It was pretty, and it was only fifty cents. I took it home, washed it, and looked at it under the light. A few months later I took it to a jeweler to ask what kind of stone it had. He checked it out and told me the ring was worth about three hundred dollars. How exciting! The best part was telling my friends about it. I was experiencing serendipity.

Experts say that most of us have valuable articles in our possession that we are unaware of. Maybe something tucked away in the attic or basement would bring a good price from a collector.

Today we're not heading for the garage or attic to look for hidden treasures. Our treasure chest is within easy reach. It's in the Book! There is no end to the wealth we have in Christ.

1. According to Psalm 104:24, what is the earth full of?

2. What is one of the treasures God gives to us (Deuteronomy 28:12)?

3. What is the price of a virtuous woman (Proverbs 31:10)?

4. What is more valuable than silver and gold (Proverbs 3:13, 14)?

5. Name some valuable things we enjoy.

6. If we honor the Lord with our offering, what does God promise (Malachi 3:10)?

7. What hidden treasure do Proverbs 2:3 and 4 mention?

8. According to Proverbs 1:7, what is the starting point of knowledge?

9. God's Word is certainly an important treasure. What does it provide to us (Psalm 119:105)?

10. According to Psalm 118:24, why should we rejoice?

11. Psalm 119:114 mentions two truths about God that are precious to us. What are they? What third precious thing does the verse mention?

12. According to Psalm 68:19, with what does God load us daily?

13. Read Psalm 103:2. What are we commanded to do?

14. Believers in Jesus Christ have been blessed with spiritual riches beyond measure. Read the following verses and note what they say about our spiritual riches.

Ephesians 1:7

Ephesians 1:18

Ephesians 2:7

Ephesians 3:16

Ephesians 3:8

15. What kind of benefits are waiting for those who love the Lord (1 Corinthians 2:9)?

16. While we wait for those heavenly benefits, what should "dwell in [us] richly" according to Colossians 3:16?

17. What are some practical ways to discover and enjoy the riches of God's Word?

It is easy to get caught up in temporal things. While some of them may be valuable, none of them have eternal value. We need to be reminded of the words of the Lord Jesus: "Lay not up for yourselves treasures upon earth, where moth and rust doth corrupt, and where thieves break through and steal: But lay up for yourselves treasures in heaven, where neither moth nor rust doth corrupt, and where thieves do not break through nor steal. For where your treasure is, there will your heart be also" (Matthew 6:19–21). Each of us needs to ask the question, Where is my heart?

The riches we have in Christ are too numerous to count. The best is yet to come. "The things which are seen are temporal; but the things which are not seen are eternal" (2 Corinthians 4:18).

Just consider . . .

Heirs with Christ (Romans 8:16, 17)
A heavenly mansion (John 14:2)
The peace of God (John 14:27)
Joy unspeakable (1 Peter 1:8)
An incorruptible, undefiled inheritance (1 Peter 1:4)
Eternal life (John 10:28)!

Can you add to the list?

Rehearsing the riches we have in Christ is a great pick-me-up and is a key factor in maintaining balance in a stress-filled world.

God Is Big Enough

H E WAS A RICH MAN. There was nothing on earth he couldn't buy. Everything in his life was perfect. He had a big family. His wife and children were happy and healthy. His house was magnificent. He enjoyed entertaining large crowds. Things couldn't have been better—*until* . . .

The messenger approached anxiously. "Sir we've been robbed. Everything was taken. I'm the only one who survived."

Before he finished his sentence, another messenger entered the room. "There's been a fire on the ranch. All the animals are dead, and even the ranch hands were killed. I'm the only survivor."

The wealthy man reeled with the disastrous news. Before the second messenger had finished with his horrendous news, another messenger entered the room. "There's been an accident!" he cried. "Your children were together at a party, and the house was destroyed. They're all dead."

Could things get any worse? The man's grief was unbearable. Then he suddenly came down with a horrible disease. He was covered from head to toe in unbearable boils. Was he crushed? Could he survive the tragedy? The answer is found in the book of Job. "Naked came I out of my mother's womb, and naked shall I return thither: the LORD gave, and the LORD hath taken away; blessed be the name of the LORD. In all this Job sinned not, nor charged God foolishly" (Job 1:21, 22).

What problem in your life seems insurmountable? Are there mountains too big to climb? Are you at a place in your life where you feel trapped with no way to turn?

One day Kathy was at that point in her life when a godly Sunday School teacher asked, "Is God big enough to resolve your problems?" That question put all her anxiety into perspective.

How Big Is God?

God created the universe (Genesis 1:1–7).

God put the stars in place (Psalm 147:4).

God created mankind (Genesis 1:27; 2:21, 22).

God knows all (Psalm 139:2, 3).

God sees all (Proverbs 15:3).

There is only one conclusion: God is powerful enough to solve any problem.

God's Power in the Old Testament

Jehoiachin, the last reigning king of Judah, was in a precarious situation. His kingdom had been besieged by Nebuchadnezzar. There didn't seem to be any hope for his family or him (2 Kings 24:12–15).

King Nebuchadnezzar made Jehoiachin's uncle, Mattaniah, the king in his place and changed Mattaniah's name to Zedekiah. While Jehoiachin was being held in prison, his relative ran the country.

1. Zedekiah rebelled against Babylon. What was the result of his rebellion (2 Kings 24:20; 25:7)?

2. Jehoiachin seemed to be in a terrible position. What did God do to reveal His power to Jehoiachin (2 Kings 25:27–30)?

3. How do 2 Kings 24:8 and 9 describe Jehoiachin?

4. Even though Jehoiachin was not a good king, God had a purpose in preserving him. Scan Matthew 1:11–16. What do you think that purpose was? (Note: "Jechonias" in verse 11 is Jehoiachin.)

God had promised Eve that one day the Seed of the woman would bruise the head of the serpent, Satan (Genesis 3:15). In addition, God promised David that his seed would have an eternal throne (2 Samuel 7:12–16). By using a heathen king, Nebuchadnezzar of Babylon, to preserve Jehoiachin's life and line, God could send His Son, of the seed of David, centuries later. Our God is powerful enough to fulfill His promises!

5. What do Psalm 75:6 and 7 tell us about God's power?

Consider another Old Testament example.

6. How was God's power evident in the life of Daniel (Daniel 6:1–23)?

Finding yourself in a den of lions would be a bad situation. However, God took care of Daniel, and He can take care of you.

The book of Daniel records another situation, which, by any measure, is high on the stress meter. Three Hebrew men were thrown into a furnace with flames so hot that they killed the soldiers who threw them in (Daniel 3:1–22).

7. How were the Hebrew men preserved (Daniel 3:23–28)?

God's Power in the New Testament

The Gospels record many times when the disciples observed the power of the Son of God.

8. Summarize the account in Mark 4:37–41, which is one example of Jesus' power.

A man had been running from the law since he was a child. He was a bad man. He acted as if he had the right to take what belonged to others. No one showed him compassion, and he didn't need anyone—until the day he came to the end of himself. He had no hope, and his life was doomed. It was the worst day of his life. He had only a few moments left to live, and then he met the Savior. His sentence wasn't lifted; he still met his doom on earth, but he received the priceless gift of eternal life because he believed on the Lord Jesus Christ. The worst day of his life became the best day of his life. We don't know his name, but his last moments are recorded in Luke 23:32–43.

9. Christ bestowed a gift to a hardened criminal before He Himself died on the cross. How did this forgiveness show the power of God? Read Jesus' words in Luke 5:18–25.

10. What is perhaps the signature event of all history that displayed God's power? Read Ephesians 1:19 and 20.

God's Power on Our Behalf

11. From Whom do Christ's followers get power to be His witnesses since He has ascended to Heaven? Read Acts 1:8.

12. Satan, our enemy, is a powerful angel. How do we know that God is more powerful? Read Job 1:12 and 2:6.

13. As we submit to our powerful God, what will happen according to James 4:7?

14. According to 1 Corinthians 6:14 and 2 Corinthians 4:14, what will God's power one day do for us?

God is big enough to rule the universe, yet none of your troubles is too small for you to take to Him. "Are not two sparrows sold for a farthing? and one of them shall not fall on the ground without your Father. But the very hairs of your head are all numbered" (Matthew 10:29, 30).

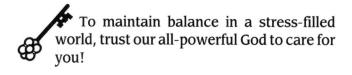 To maintain balance in a stress-filled world, trust our all-powerful God to care for you!

Conclusion

THE PURPOSE OF these ten lessons has been to discover from God's Word the keys for maintaining spiritual balance in a stress-filled world. Here is a summary of the ten keys. You may want to copy this list and carry it with you or post it where you will see it frequently. When the stress comes—and it will—use these keys to maintain your spiritual balance.

Ten Keys to Maintaining Balance in a Stress-filled World
1. Place your struggles into God's hands.
2. Trust God to be your strength.
3. Remember that your relationship to God is eternal.
4. Ask God to help you guard your heart, mind, and tongue.
5. Remind yourself that your hope is in Christ.
6. Pray, knowing God is listening.
7. Remember that you are held in the palm of God's hand.
8. Learn not to dwell on if-onlys and what-ifs.
9. Rehearse the riches you have in Christ.
10. Trust the all-powerful God to care for you.

LEADER'S GUIDE

Suggestions for Leaders

The effectiveness of a group Bible study usually depends on two things: (1) the leader herself and (2) the ladies' commitment to prepare beforehand and interact during the study. You cannot totally control the second factor, but you have total control over the first one. These brief suggestions will help you be an effective Bible study leader.

You will want to prepare each lesson a week in advance. During the week, read supplemental material and look for illustrations in the everyday events of your life as well as in the lives of others.

Encourage the ladies in the Bible study to complete each lesson before the meeting itself. This preparation will make the discussion more interesting. You can suggest that ladies answer two or three questions a day as part of their daily Bible reading time rather than trying to do the entire lesson at one sitting.

The physical setting in which you meet will have some bearing on the study itself. An informal circle of chairs, chairs around a table, someone's living room or family room—these types of settings encourage people to relax and participate. In addition to an informal setting, create an atmosphere in which ladies feel free to participate and be themselves.

During the discussion time, here are a few things to observe:

• Don't do all the talking. This is not designed to be a lecture.

• Encourage discussion on each question by adding ideas and questions.

• Don't discuss controversial issues that will divide the group. (Differences of opinion are healthy; divisions are not.)

• Don't allow one lady to dominate the discussion. Use statements such as these to draw others into the study: "Let's hear from someone on this side of the room" (the side opposite the dominant talker); "Let's hear from someone who has not shared yet today."

• Stay on the subject. The tendency toward tangents is always possible in a discussion. One of your responsibilities as the leader is to keep the group on track.

• Don't get bogged down on a question that interests only one person.

You may want to use the last fifteen minutes of the scheduled time for prayer. If you have a large group of ladies, divide into smaller groups for prayer. You could call this the "Share and Care Time."

If you have a morning Bible study, encourage the ladies to go out for lunch with someone else from time to time. This is a good way to get acquainted with new ladies. Occasionally you could plan a time when ladies bring their own lunches or salads to share and eat together. These things help promote fellowship and friendship in the group.

The formats that follow are suggestions only. You can plan your own format, use one of these, or adapt one of these to your needs.

2-hour Bible Study
10:00—10:15   Coffee and fellowship time
10:15—10:30   Get-acquainted time
Have two ladies take five minutes each to tell something about themselves and their families.
Also use this time to make announcements and, if appropriate, take an offering for the babysitters.
10:30—11:45   Bible study
Leader guides discussion of the questions in the day's lesson.
11:45—12:00   Prayer time

2-hour Bible Study
10:00—10:45   Bible lesson
Leader teaches a lesson on the content of the material. No discussion during this time.
10:45—11:00   Coffee and fellowship
11:00—11:45   Discussion time
Divide into small groups with an appointed leader for each group. Discuss the questions in the day's lesson.
11:45—12:00   Prayer time

1½-hour Bible Study
10:00—10:30   Bible study
Leader guides discussion of half the questions in the day's lesson.
10:30—10:45   Coffee and fellowship
10:45—11:15   Bible study
Leader continues discussion of the questions in the day's lesson.
11:15—11:30   Prayer time

Answers for Leader's Use

Information inside parentheses ( ) is additional instruction for the group leader.

Lesson 1
1. God promised never to leave us or forsake us.
2. Some examples are Moses, Joseph, Ruth, David, Daniel, Esther.
3. When we are tempted, God is there to provide a way of escape. He gives us grace, or unmerited divine assistance, to bear our burdens.
4. She could feel depressed or bitter or angry.
5. When we are out of balance, we display anger. We overreact to everyday situations. We can't control our emotions, and we are too sensitive.
6. When our life is out of balance, we need to go to the One Who created

us. He knows everything about us. Sometimes the problem could be our health. We need to ask for wisdom. Most important, we must commit each day to the Lord.

7. Possible answers include when David fought Goliath; when he had to run from Saul; when Jonathan died; after his sin with Bathsheba; when friends betrayed him.

8. Time, freedom, sleep, the respect of others, and her own self-respect.

9. Personal answers. (Let the group members share what they consider important truths. A few suggestions are God loves us; He sent His Son to die for us; He knows our pain and cares about us; He understands us.)

10. When we focus on ourselves, we become selfish. When we focus on the needs of others, we become more loving. When we focus on Christ, we become more Christlike.

11. If we don't take time to grieve, our loss and grief will affect us in ways we may not recognize. Our grief can cause us to flare up at something unrelated. Relationships can be pulled apart for flimsy reasons. Feelings of stress and anger crop up inexplicably. These are common occurrences for people who won't allow themselves to grieve.

12. God does care about the details of our lives (see Matthew 10:29–31), but He is even more concerned with how we respond to those details. Are we allowing the things that happen to us to make us more like Christ?

13. God provided for Elijah by sending ravens with bread and meat. (Ask the ladies to think of others in the Bible who had needs. How did God provide? Two examples are God's preservation of Moses [Exod. 2:1–10] and God's care for Shadrach, Meshach, and Abed-nego [Dan. 3:9–30].)

14. True, honest, just, pure, lovely, of good report, virtuous, praiseworthy.

15. True joy is a fruit the Holy Spirit produces in us when we have a right relationship with God.

16. We can maintain joy by making sure our lives are right before God so that the Holy Spirit can work in us. Daily prayer and Bible study are important ingredients in our relationship with the Lord.

17. Focus on heavenly things (things of eternal value) rather than on earthly, material things (things that have only temporal value).

18. The kinds of thoughts that delight God are those that honor Him. People should think about and "glory in" (i.e., rejoice in) understanding and knowing God, because He exercises "lovingkindness, judgment, and righteousness."

Lesson 2

1. John 3:16—God the Father showed His love by giving His Son. Galatians 2:20—God the Son revealed His love by giving Himself to pay for our sins.

2. To prevent bitterness from growing in our lives, we must watch diligently for things like pride, animosity, or rivalry that could grow into bitterness.
3. Personal answers. (Ask ladies to share their answers. The basic idea is that God promises to be there for us, to provide strength and courage when we need it.)
4. God loves us. His Son died for our sins. He will give eternal life to all who believe.
5. Jesus came to give eternal life ("I am come that they might have life") and an abundant, full life ("and that they might have it more abundantly").
6. Sin.
7. Death.
8. To access the abundant life, we must start with what God wants us to do. 1 Timothy 2:5—We must accept Christ; He is the "mediator between God and men." 1 Peter 3:18—We must trust in Christ, for He alone suffered for our sins to "bring us to God." Romans 5:8—God loved us. Even though we were sinners, Christ died for us. John 1:12—We must receive Christ. Everyone who receives Him has the power to become the sons (children) of God. Romans 10:9—Confess with our mouths the Lord Jesus and believe in our hearts that God raised Him from the dead. That's how we are saved; that's how we access the abundant life. Acts 16:31—Believe on the Lord Jesus Christ.
9. We can turn boldly to God; He offers mercy and grace to help in time of need.
10. There's no way God can abandon us, because we are in the hand of the Son (v. 28) and of the Father (v. 29). No one (not even we ourselves) can pluck us out of His hands.
11. His ways are not our ways, and His ways are past finding out.
12. For those who love God, He works all things together for good.
13. Strength.
14. Christ.
15. The promise that Christ has gone away to Heaven to prepare a place for us comforts us. He is preparing a place for us to spend that eternal life He has given us!
16. Momentary; glory; seen; temporary; eternal.
17. We sorrow, but not as those who have no hope.
18. Walk; redeem; understand; be filled; speak, thanks.
19. Warn; comfort, or encourage; support, or help; patient; evil, evil; good; rejoice; pray; give thanks.

Lesson 3
1. Philippians 1:20—Melissa could learn to magnify Christ with her body. Philippians 1:27—Melissa should conduct herself in a way that would not detract from the gospel of Christ. Philippians 4:8—Melissa

needed to think about things that were true, honest, just, pure, lovely, good, virtuous, and praiseworthy.
2. Personal answers. (Discuss some reasons for church attendance.)
3. The reason to come together in worship is to provoke (motivate) each other to love and good works and to exhort (encourage) one another.
4. It shouldn't be our only reason.
5. Second Timothy 1:9 points out that God saved us for His own purpose and according to His grace, not our work (anything we've done). So when we use our talents in church, we are not adding to our merit. We were saved and are accepted by God's grace. If we're trying to earn merit with God through our efforts, we have misunderstood His grace. However, our good works reflect the holy life we're living by His grace.
6. Mercy; works.
7. We should forgive. Don't let someone's actions rob you of joy. Forgive for your own benefit, not for the benefit of the one who has offended (Eph. 4:32).
8. It tells us to forgive others as Christ forgave us.
9. God. It makes us God's fellow workers.
10. Worthy. Every good work.
11. Works; pleasure, or purpose.
12. Good works.
13. Not works we do to save us, but works we do because we are saved.
14. (List the ladies' answers on a chalkboard or whiteboard.)
15. Personal answers. (Discuss the possibility of a needy family, a missionary family, or someone else for whom the group as a whole could do kind deeds.)
16. By committing our thought life to Christ every day. As soon as we think a wrong thought, we need to confess it and bring it into captivity to the obedience of Christ.

Lesson 4

1. Holy. Grace to help us.
2. Possible answers include the following ideas: Mature Christian women are prayer warriors and teachers; many have a ministry with children; they are servants (e.g., they prepare food for the bereaved); they counsel; they have wisdom and experience in child-rearing and family matters. They don't gossip; they encourage and praise instead of criticize and complain; they're gentle, even in rebuking; they don't talk about what they've done for others and the Lord; they're not judgmental. They're self-sacrificing, but you won't hear that from them. They're deliberate, not impulsive.
3. What holy behavior looks like; how not to be false accusers; how to be good teachers; how to love our husbands and children; how to be

discreet and chaste; how to love our own husbands.

4. New; the Creator's.

5. Thanksgiving.

6. Always with grace, seasoned with salt.

7. Nothing corrupt or worthless should come out of our mouths. What we do say should be useful in edifying (building up, encouraging) others. We should talk this way because it is becoming to God, to Whom we now belong.

8. Words reveal the inner person (Matt. 12:34). Uplifting, pleasant speech honors the Lord; gossip and other sins of the tongue dishonor Him.

9. So he wouldn't be ashamed, and so that Christ would be magnified.

10. By putting on the armor of God: truth, righteousness, peace, faith, salvation, and the sword of the Lord. If we're "wearing" these, our thoughts and words will be appropriate and will please God.

11. No. Weigh your words to see if they are better left unsaid.

12. Guard our minds (v. 23); "dress ourselves" with righteousness and holiness (v. 24); determine to speak the truth, not lies (v. 25); don't let anger lead to speech problems (v. 26); practice the use of edifying speech (v. 29); rely on the Spirit (v. 30); be kind and forgiving (v. 32).

13. Each of us alone is responsible for what she has done. (Christ will reward us accordingly.) No one can make you be aggressive, mean, angry, bitter. You *choose* to be ruled by those responses.

14. There is a way of escape from any temptation. In regard to speech, pray, change the subject, end the conversation. Some suggestions: "Talking about this makes me uncomfortable. Can we talk about something else?" Or say something positive. These are nonthreatening ways of directing the conversation to more God-honoring topics. Gossiping is discussing a situation in which you either are not involved or cannot be part of the solution to the problem.

15. Making his words acceptable to God.

Lesson 5

1. Nathan let David know that God had forgiven David and that David would not die.

2. His child died.

3. God doesn't deal with us according to our sins; rather, He deals in mercy.

4. So we'll trust Him instead of ourselves.

5. Not always. The actions of others or circumstances beyond our control might cause us pain.

6. Unresolved conflict in relationships with children, mates, and friends; the world situation; poverty; health; job situations; crime.

7. God was with him and showed him mercy.

8. He cared for the needs of others. He recognized God's sovereignty in all things.
9. Personal answers. (Ask if one or two volunteers would be willing to share their answers.)
10. Pray, read Scripture, see a Christian counselor, talk to friends.
11. We can ask God for wisdom in dealing with our pain. If emotional pain is caused by an unforgiving spirit, we must deal with that.
12. We don't want to share our pain. Sometimes we feel it is too personal to talk about.
13. So God can glorify Himself through us.
14. Cast our burdens on the Lord. He has promised to sustain us. He will not allow us to be moved.
15. When we come to Him with our burdens, He gives rest.

Lesson 6

1. Answers will vary. Some examples are Hannah, who prayed for a child (1 Sam. 1:10, 11, 20); Daniel, who prayed for wisdom to know the king's dream (Dan. 2:17–23); the early church prayed for Peter (Acts 12:1–16).
2. No. He knows what is best for us, so sometimes His answer is no or wait; it is not always yes.
3. Yes. But she was so excited that she forgot to let him in.
4. Answers may vary. One possible explanation is because they were not praying for his release. They may have been praying that he would be bold and not forsake the Lord, even if it meant death. If they were not praying for his release, they certainly would not expect him to be at the door.
5. It may have been easier to believe an angel was at the door, given the unlikely event that Peter would get out of prison.
6. Share the news.
7. (Ask several ladies to share their answers. Ask: How does answered prayer strengthen your faith?)
8. Personal answers. (Ask volunteers to answer.)
9. By keeping constant contact with God and not allowing ourselves to drift away from the open line of communication. The access is immediate anytime.
10. To obtain mercy and grace for the time of need.
11. In prayer.
12. That his faith would not fail.
13. So they wouldn't enter into temptation. He said that their spirit was willing but that their flesh was weak.
14. He answered by allowing Christ to be crucified for the sins of the world.
15. The effective, fervent prayer of a believer accomplishes great things.

16. The rain stopped (1 Kings 17:1), and then the rain came again (1 Kings 18:1, 45).
17. Trust the Lord and recognize that our own understanding is limited; therefore, we shouldn't depend on it.
18. "Hallowed be thy name" (praise); "thy will be done" (submission); "give us . . . our daily bread" (requests); "forgive us our sins" (repentance); "we also forgive every one that is indebted to us" (reminder to forgive others); "lead us not into temptation" (request for victory); "deliver us from evil" (request for deliverance).

Lesson 7
1. Where He always is . . . with us. He never leaves or forsakes His own.
2. He rebelled and tried to run from God.
3. They may suffer from some of the consequences of our rebellion. The sailors experienced a bad storm because of Jonah's disobedience.
4. He was thrown overboard, and the storm stopped.
5. God sent the storm, which He would ultimately use to bring Jonah back to Himself.
6. He had prepared a big fish to swallow Jonah.
7. Praying.
8. The fish spit him up on dry ground.
9. Things don't go as we would like them to.
10. Personal answers.
11. A loving Father; spiritual food; provision for life and godliness (1 Pet. 1:3); the position as heirs (Rom. 8:17).
12. He waited for his son, watching for his return.
13. Possible answers include ask forgiveness, pray, study the Bible, seek Christian counseling.
14. Philippians 3:13—Look ahead, not back. Psalm 103:2—Rehearse all that God has done for you. Psalm 5:3—Begin each day by committing it to the Lord. 1 Thessalonians 5:18—Learn to give thanks for all things. Philippians 4:8—Think about the right things.

Lesson 8
1. Her husband and sons had died.
2. To return to their own families.
3. She left her family and country to go to Naomi's family and country and God.
4. Boaz was a relative of her husband.
5. He told her to glean only in his field (v. 8). He had the workers leave grain for her (vv. 15, 16). He ensured her safety (v. 9), and he saw to it that her needs were met (vv. 9, 14).
6. She had taken good care of Naomi.
7. He reassured her; then he went to the nearest kinsmen to redeem her.
8. He would be required to marry Ruth, and his heir would be named

after Ruth's dead husband. His own inheritance would be in jeopardy.
9. King David.
10. By the children of Ruth and Boaz.
11. Personal answers.
12. Personal answers. (Ask the ladies to share their answers. For some practical pointers on this subject, order the booklet *Helping a Friend Who Is Grieving* [RBP5295]. Call 1-800-727-4440 or your distributor; or visit RBP on-line at www.regularbaptistpress.org.)
13. Personal answers. (Ask the ladies to share their answers. For a helpful list of passages, order the booklet *Scriptures for Coping with Grief and Loss* [RBP5297]. Call 1-800-727-4440 or your distributor; or visit RBP on-line at www.regularbaptistpress.org.)
14. She had a husband who loved and cared for her. She had at least one son. She was well respected in Bethlehem.
15. Nothing is impossible with God.
16. Unbelief.

Lesson 9
1. God's riches, which He created.
2. Rain.
3. Far above rubies.
4. Wisdom.
5. Possible answers include salvation, family, air, freedom.
6. God promises to bless us. (Explain that this promise was given to Israel, and God's blessings for Israel were almost always physical in nature. The application of the passage to us would focus more on spiritual blessing.)
7. Understanding.
8. The fear of the Lord.
9. Light on the pathway of life.
10. Because God made the day.
11. God is our hiding place and our shield. His Word.
12. Benefits.
13. Not forget His benefits to us.
14. Ephesians 1:7—Redemption and forgiveness are riches of God's grace. 1:18—We can know the riches of God's glory. 2:7—God will show us the riches of His grace throughout eternity. 3:16—We are spiritually strengthened by His riches. 3:8—God's riches are unsearchable.
15. Unimaginably wonderful benefits.
16. The Word of God.
17. Read it regularly and systematically; study it; memorize it; listen to the Word of God when it is preached and taught; read devotional and study books that focus on the Word.

Lesson 10
1. His sons were killed. He watched them die before his own eyes were put out. He was left with no heirs.
2. He allowed Jehoiachin to receive honor, to eat with the king, and to receive an allowance for the rest of his life.
3. He was an evil king.
4. God preserved the line of the Messiah, fulfilling His promise for someone to sit on the throne of David forever.
5. He is the One Who sets up and disposes rulers.
6. God sent an angel to shut the lions' mouths.
7. God sent an angel who delivered the three men from the fire.
8. Christ calmed the storm by speaking to it.
9. Only God has the power to forgive sin.
10. The resurrection of Christ from the grave.
11. The Holy Spirit, Who is God.
12. Satan can do only what God allows.
13. When we submit to Him, God gives us power to resist the Devil and make him flee.
14. Raise our bodies from the grave.